★ 1,001 THINGS ★
DEMOCRATS
GET RIGHT

A COMPLETE GUIDE
—— FOR VOTERS ——

BILL O'RIGHTS

CASTLE POINT BOOKS
NEW YORK

www.stmartins.com
www.castlepointbooks.com

The Castle Point Books trademark is owned by Castle Point Publishing, LLC.
Castle Point books are published and distributed by St. Martin's Press.

ISBN 978-1-250-23530-5 (trade paperback)

Our books may be purchased in bulk for promotional, educational, or business use.
Please contact your local bookseller or the Macmillan Corporate and Premium
Sales Department at 1-800-221-7945, extension 5442, or by email
at MacmillanSpecialMarkets@macmillan.com.

First Edition: October 2019

10 9 8 7 6 5 4 3 2 1

⋆ CONTENTS ⋆

★ 1 ★

VALUES AND PRINCIPLES

VALUES AND PRINCIPLES

VALUES AND PRINCIPLES

VALUES AND PRINCIPLES

VALUES AND PRINCIPLES

★2★

OUR PLAN TO PUT AMERICA FIRST

★ 3 ★

MERITS OF
HIGHER TAXES

★ 4 ★

JOB GROWTH
STRATEGIES

★ 5 ★

WHY WORK?
THE CASE FOR GOVERNMENT HANDOUTS

★ 6 ★

HOW TO FIGHT TERRORISM

WHY WE DON'T NEED BORDERS

⋆8⋆

HOW TO PROTECT AMERICA

★9★

SOCIALISM SUCCESS STORIES

BIBLIOGRAPHY

INDEX